First published in the UK by Sweet Cherry Publishing Limited, 2022
Unit 36, Vulcan House, Vulcan Road,
Leicester, LE5 3EF, United Kingdom

Sweet Cherry Europe (Europe address)
Nauschgasse 4/3/2 POB 1017
Vienna, WI 1220, Austria

2 4 6 8 10 9 7 5 3

ISBN: 978-1-78226-893-2

© Sweet Cherry Publishing Limited 2022

Football Rising Stars: Jadon Sancho

All rights reserved. No part of this publication may be reproduced or utilised in any form or by any means, electronic or mechanical, including photocopying, recording, or using any information storage and retrieval system, without prior permission in writing from the publisher.

The right of Harry Meredith to be identified as the author of this work has been asserted by them in accordance with the Copyright, Designs and Patents Act 1988.

Text by Harry Meredith
Illustrations by Sophie Jones

Lexile® code numerical measure L = Lexile® 940L

www.sweetcherrypublishing.com

Printed in India

JADON SANCHO
THE UNOFFICIAL STORY

Written by
HARRY MEREDITH

Sweet Cherry

CONTENTS

1. Jadon's Decision	7
2. Kennington Streets	14
3. Watford Academy	22
4. From South to North	33
5. The Young Lions	42
6. The Yellow Wall	52
7. The Assist King	63
8. The Three Lions	73
9. The Champions League	84
10. Return to Manchester?	90
11. A Role Model at Dortmund	100
12. The Red Devils	111
13. Road to Qatar 2022	118

JADON'S DECISION

In the summer of 2017, Jadon was in a meeting with one of the world's most famous football managers.

Pep Guardiola.

Jadon's palms were sweaty as he sat opposite the boss, resting his hands on the arms of his chair.

'We value you, Jadon,' said Guardiola, leaning forwards in his trademark grey round-neck sweater and white undershirt.

'I know you do,' said Jadon. 'But I need to play.'

'And you will soon.' Guardiola raised his hands in the air. 'Look at where you are,' he said, getting up from his seat and pointing to the training ground outside the window. 'You are a football player for Manchester City. Living the dream of millions of kids around the world. You train with the best talent. The very best talent.'

★ JADON SANCHO ★

Jadon held the pen in his hand and looked down at the contract before him. A contract that would earn him £35,000 a week at the age of 17. A contract that would see him continue to learn and develop with some of football's best players.

Jadon saw himself setting up assists for Sergio Agüero, playing one-twos with Kevin De Bruyne and sprinting down the opposite wing to Raheem Sterling. But in those visions, it was still only in training. Jadon hadn't yet played a single first-team minute.

 ★ FOOTBALL RISING STARS ★

He would likely be spending the first few years of his new contract keeping the bench warm, or even worse playing for the under 23s. No matter what Guardiola said, the truth was that it was hard for home-grown talent to make it in the Premier League. Especially at a club with millions of pounds worth of talent.

'I can't sign it,' said Jadon, putting the pen down and rising from his seat.

'If you do not sign, we will not be taking you to America with us for the pre-season tour,' said Guardiola.

★ JADON SANCHO ★

Jadon looked at him and sighed. He had been looking forward to a summer of beaches, sun and sport.

Jadon walked to the door and opened it. 'Thank you for everything,' he said.

A man used to getting what he wanted, Guardiola stood there in disbelief as Jadon closed the door behind him. In the near future, he would be closing the door on his time at Manchester City too.

This was the decision that set Jadon Sancho's career in motion. Not long after this fateful meeting, one of the biggest clubs in the German Bundesliga put in an offer for him. Borussia Dortmund, keen to tempt talented young British players overseas, sent a bid of £8 million. This was a risky decision for Jadon. He'd be leaving his home country and living somewhere completely alien to him, where he didn't understand the language. It would be a career path rarely taken by the thousands of players who had came before him. But what mattered to Jadon was that at Borussia Dortmund he would have a chance to play first-team football.

★ JADON SANCHO ★

So he said yes.

It was a decision that would turn him from a bit-part academy player into one of the world's most talented young football players.

2
KENNINGTON STREETS

Jadon has spent most of his footballing career in the city of Manchester and overseas in Germany. But it's the city of London where you'll find his home.

Jadon Malik Sancho was born on the 25th of March 2000, and raised by parents who had moved to

⭐ JADON SANCHO ⭐

England from Trinidad and Tobago. Jadon grew up in Kennington, South London, and in this busy urban area, he was forced to learn his footballing skills and tricks on the streets. In fact, on the estate where he grew up, there was a large sign stating 'No Ball Games'. Thankfully for the world of football, Jadon ignored that sign.

Worried about her son playing on the roads, Jadon's mother signed him up for a community project. The project was aimed at giving young city kids a place to play football away from the chaos and crime in the area. It was an outlet for kids that helped to steer them away from people who might tempt them into making poor life choices. It was in this community project that 'cages', as they're known locally, were brought into the borough. They were small tarmacked playgrounds surrounded by a metal fence.

One day, Jadon's coach, with a ball tucked under his arm, opened the gate and the kids charged into the playground.

'I want ten laps,' he shouted.

⭐ JADON SANCHO ⭐

Jadon and his friends, with their seemingly endless energy, zipped around the cage with smiles beaming from their faces. Jadon, with his natural pace, was soon leading the pack. He even lapped some of his friends.

'Thanks for coming, everyone,' said the coach. 'Today it's all about end-to-end football. I want to see one touch, two touch. Don't hog the ball. Pass it quickly. Move your feet and think fast.'

This format of close-quarter football had produced plenty of talent throughout the years.

Having to make your way out of tight spaces, without the width and length of a football pitch, encouraged players to keep possession and try creative new tricks to get past their opponents.

It wasn't just football skills that Jadon learnt from the project. It helped kids in the local area develop as people too. The project provided them with a free, fun and beneficial experience outside of the classroom.

'Pass it, Jadon!' shouted one of his friends. Jadon darted across the playground with the ball so close to his feet that you'd think it was stuck to them with glue. He hit the ball against the wall as if he were playing FIFA Street, and it rebounded through the goalkeeper's legs. The ball fell to his friend, leaving an open goal for an easy tap in.

'Megs!' everyone shouted. The goalkeeper held his hand over his eyes and let out an embarrassed laugh.

It was this brand of caged football, created by the community playground project, that produced the likes of Manchester United legend Rio Ferdinand, and other talents such as Ademola Lookman and Reiss Nelson. In fact, Jadon and Nelson grew up playing together. Although they did not play football in the same cage at first, word spread about these two talented young players. Soon they were brought together to play in local youth tournaments. In one of these tournaments, the pair managed to score twenty-four goals together in just ten matches. It was performances like these that started to grab the attention of local scouts.

★ JADON SANCHO ★

At the age of just 7, Jadon was offered the chance to play at Watford FC's professional academy.

3
WATFORD ACADEMY

Jadon stared out of the car window at the red light ahead.

'We're going to be late,' he huffed, leaning on the window.

'We'll make it,' said the taxi driver. 'Don't you worry.'

One of the first sacrifices Jadon

had to make for his footballing career was leaving his family home. With Watford's training academy on the opposite side of London, the daily commute just wasn't practical. So Jadon moved in with his aunt in Northolt.

The Watford Academy had a lot of development centres in and around London. They would often find 'street football players' and bring them in to see if they had what it took to play organised football.

Jadon hopped out of the taxi, making sure to remember his boot bag.

'Thanks,' he said to the driver, before rushing to the entrance. Standing by the gate, in his Watford tracksuit, was the coach waiting to welcome him.

Jadon followed him into the centre. He'd never seen so many football pitches. There were matches being played on each one. Some with young kids, and others with older teenagers. Every player was striving to stand out and be the one to make it.

Arriving at the club at such a young age, Jadon hadn't yet had the chance

⋆✶ JADON SANCHO ✶⋆

to test himself in an 11 vs 11 game. To see how he'd fare, the coaches at Watford placed him with an age group two years above him.

'This is Jadon,' said the coach to the rest of the team. A couple of the players nodded and waved, while the rest quite simply ignored him. It was clear that he was younger than they were, and they didn't see him as a threat to their position. The coach blew the whistle and the training game began.

Jadon was on the left wing and darted into a space.

'I'm free! I'm free!' he shouted, but the players ignored his calls. After a few minutes, the ball found its way to Jadon's feet, and he made the most of his opportunity. The other kids may have been older, and physically stronger, but they never had a chance of getting near the ball. Jadon kept it tucked into his feet and danced through the opposition. With each touch, his confidence grew. He swooped in between two defenders, leaving them kicking at nothing but air, before finding his way to the corner of the box to curl in a pinpoint cross.

⭐ JADON SANCHO ⭐

The attacker on his side got his head to it, but it grazed the crossbar and went out for a goal kick. The

older players placed their hands on their hips and looked at one another in shock.

This kid had talent!

In the following years, Jadon signed his first schoolboy contract. On the day of the signing, the coach at Watford was scared that someone from Arsenal or Chelsea would try to tempt Jadon to join their club instead. So he picked Jadon and his family up at the train station and drove them to the training ground himself.

Jadon was later offered his school's boarding programme. This meant that he would be able to stay at Harefield Academy during the week and cut out the taxi journeys from Northolt. This allowed him to spend more time on the training pitch and less in London traffic.

From Monday to Friday Jadon had school at the academy. His  days involved a mix of schoolwork and training sessions, allowing him to receive both a schooling and footballing education. It was an intense workload in pursuit of his goal: a constant cycle of practice, practice and you guessed it … *practice*.

However, even during his school lessons, Jadon's mind would often be on football.

Early one morning, Jadon was in a lesson. The kids had their laptops out on their desks and were supposed to be using them to work, but Jadon had other plans. Instead of solving sums or researching, Jadon was on YouTube watching videos of his icon Ronaldinho – a Brazilian legend known for his incredible skill and technique.

Jadon spent hours watching his idol pull off countless turns and tricks that made defenders look like they'd never played the game before. It was this flair and ability that had a huge influence on Jadon's style of play. He didn't just want to beat a defender: he wanted to trick them in the most skilful way he could.

Jadon developed his craft at Watford for over seven years. He grew from a young player having a kick about with his friends, to a teenage trickster with the potential to go professional.

During one midweek match against Arsenal, Jadon stunned onlookers with a goal of jaw-dropping brilliance. At Arsenal's Hale End Academy, Jadon collected the ball near the halfway line and sprinted between two defenders. The Arsenal youngsters were left metres away and could do nothing as he unleashed a thirty-five-yard shot that rocketed into the top corner. Moments like these were becoming more frequent.

★ **FOOTBALL RISING STARS** ★

By the age of 14, Jadon was already playing for Watford's under 18s.

This quick development caught the eye of Manchester City, and they made a rumoured initial offer of £66,000 to bring Jadon up north to play for their academy. The offer arrived at the right time for Jadon, as he believed this would be the step up he needed to improve. He was also excited by the opportunity to get out of his home city, and away from the distractions of the bustling capital.

4

FROM SOUTH TO NORTH

When stories first started to spread that Manchester City were interested in Jadon, he hardly gave them a thought. He had lived in London all his life and at that point it was hard to imagine a team as decorated as Manchester City showing interest. He dismissed the talk as rumours.

But they were certainly more than rumours. Manchester City, now a dominant force in the English game, saw a gem in Jadon. They wanted to steal the 14-year-old away from Watford.

In footballing terms, it was clear that Manchester City were performing at a higher level than Watford. But it would involve another move – this time from the south of the country to the north. However, knowing the career path and story behind Raheem Sterling, one of Manchester City's top talents at the time, convinced Jadon that this would be the right decision.

Like Jadon, Sterling had grown up in London. Instead of Watford, his career had started at Queens Park Rangers, and the initial interest to bring him up north was from Liverpool. Sterling then went on to become one of the country's best players. In 2015 he was sold to Manchester City for a mouth-watering

fee of £44 million. At the time, this was the most expensive transfer for an English player. Not only that, Sterling was now a capped and important member of the English national team.

Although Jadon tried to keep it at the back of his mind, becoming a professional and playing for the first team was his main ambition. Like every young football fan, it would be a dream come true to wear the shirt of his national team.

At first the rise in quality was hard to get to grips with at Manchester City.

⭐ JADON SANCHO ⭐

Like at Watford, Jadon often played with older age groups. It was difficult adjusting to playing with players who were older, stronger and more experienced. However, after a short while, Jadon started to grow in confidence and was given his chance to play.

In Jadon's first game for the Manchester City academy, he wore number 11. He was wearing the team's famous sky blue and playing on the left wing against Newcastle United. Within the first five minutes, the ball was, played to Jadon on the edge of the penalty box. He feinted to go down the left side before turning inside, leaving the defender helpless. He rifled the ball into the near post. The goalkeeper dove to the ground and got a hand to it, but could not prevent the ball from rippling against the back of the net. *Goal!* Jadon's teammates ran to congratulate him.

But he wasn't done yet.

Later in the game, Jadon found himself in a similar position, but there was no need to feint this time. *Boom!* He shot into the bottom left-hand corner and grabbed a brace on his academy debut. He ran away with his arms out by his sides and celebrated.

Fast forward a few months, and Jadon was relaxing with a couple of friends. He'd settled into life up north and was starting to feel at home. He felt his phone vibrating in his pocket, so he pulled it out while his friends talked among themselves. He opened the message and couldn't stop himself from smiling:

> *Jadon Sancho. You've been selected to train with the first team.*

Jadon passed his phone to his friends, and they started jumping around in excitement. He grabbed his phone back and rang those special to him. He called his mum and dad who were very proud. He was going to train with the stars of the club and learn from one of the best managers in world football: Pep Guardiola.

The incredible performances Jadon had put on at Watford were not one-offs or luck. No matter what club he played for, it was clear that he was going to succeed. The coaches at Manchester City were taking notice of this. And it wasn't just clubs that were noticing Sancho. His performances were catching the attention of the national team's manager too ...

5
THE YOUNG LIONS

Playing at Manchester City's celebrated academy certainly didn't do Jadon any harm in regard to his national team dream. While at the academy, he was selected to join up with the England U16s. There he would play alongside some of the

country's other young talent. Players such as Phil Foden, Rhian Brewster and Morgan Gibbs-White.

Despite joining up with other talented players, Jadon was still a stand-out star. He was frequently involved with goals and assists in the eleven games he played for this age group. His performances at this level earned him a spot in the U17s European Championship squad.

The team would end up bulldozing through the group stages. Jadon put in some top performances and grabbed three goals in the process.

He was the deciding player in the quarter-final, as his long-range wonder strike against the Republic of Ireland ensured a 1-0 win and progression to the semi-finals. England went on to face Turkey, and ended up beating them 2-1, setting up a challenging final against Spain.

The whistle blew and the game kicked off. England were wearing their traditional white strip and Spain their vibrant red. It was by far the biggest crowd of the tournament. The 10,000-capacity stadium in Varaždin, Croatia was filled with fans excited

★ JADON SANCHO ★

to watch some of the world's hottest footballing prospects.

Seventeen minutes into the match, Jadon was on the ball. He ran forwards halfway into the opposition's half. His teammate Callum Hudson-Odoi made a run ahead of him, and Jadon slotted it neatly into his path. Hudson-Odoi unleashed a fearsome strike that flew across the pitch and into the top right-hand corner. *Goal!* Jadon punched the air and ran after his teammate who slid on his knees into the corner flag. But it was still early.

There was a lot of football still to be played.

In fact after ninety minutes, the game was tied at 2-2. Spain had grabbed an equalising goal with hardly a second to spare. The match went to extra time followed by penalties, and the Spaniards ended up as winners. Although the national team, did not get their hands on the top prize, Jadon received praise from across the globe. With his impressive tally of goals, assists and dazzling performances, he was named the Player of the Tournament. It was from

★ JADON SANCHO ★

this point onwards that Jadon became not just a rising national star, but a player with international recognition.

Returning to Manchester City, on the back of a Player of the Tournament performance, Jadon's confidence could not have been higher. So high in fact, that later on in the season, he refused to sign the professional contract at Manchester City. Guardiola could not promise him the playing time he needed. Hardly a year had passed since the exciting text inviting him to train with the first team had arrived. Yet now he was turning down a professional contract with one of the best teams in Europe, let alone England.

Jadon's international appearances had drawn the attention of scouts across most major European leagues, and it wasn't long before Borussia Dortmund came calling. The German club's insistence on improving young players and giving them first-team experience was a key factor in the decision. Dortmund's tradition of development by playing was music to Jadon's ears, and he soon accepted their offer.

★ JADON SANCHO ★

It was a reality. Jadon Sancho could now say that he was a professional football player! However, before he could concentrate on life in the yellow and black of Dortmund, the Young Lions would need him once again.

It was time for the U17 World Cup.

Jadon flew with the rest of the young team to Kolkata in India. He put in three strong performances in the group stages, where he scored three goals and had the local fans mesmerised by the way he played. However, with the German season underway, Dortmund decided to call

Jadon back to their team. In their eyes he was ready to be playing first-team football in front of tens of thousands. Jadon, of course, felt a mixture of sadness and delight. It was a special campaign in India. However, it was not very often that a player at his age would get such an incredible opportunity to play first-team football.

Despite Jadon's departure, the Young Lions went on to progress all the way to the final of the World Cup. They avenged their previous loss by defeating Spain 5-2, coming back from being 2-0 down to win the tie.

★ JADON SANCHO ★

Jadon's former Manchester City teammate Phil Foden went on to receive the Golden Ball: an award given for the best player at the tournament. Rhian Brewster, meanwhile, was awarded the Golden Boot: an award given to the top goalscorer of the competition.

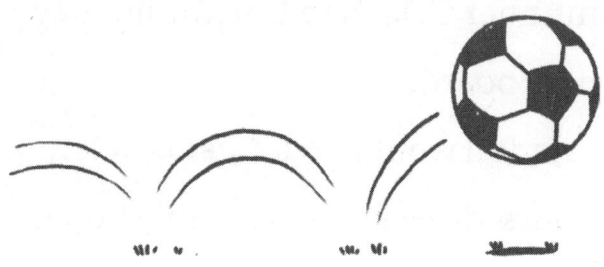

6
THE YELLOW WALL

'First class passengers for flight number GD495 to Dortmund may now board.'

Jadon would no longer be a few hours' drive from his family home

✦ JADON SANCHO ✦

in London. Instead, he was taking an international flight to another country, and the German city of Dortmund.

While Jadon was arriving in the city, another young star was on the way out. Ousame Dembélé, a player tipped to rival Kylian Mbappé (and potentially an heir to the thrones of Cristiano Ronaldo and Lionel Messi) was departing. He had been sold by Dortmund for a fee of €105 million. This had left an open spot in the team for Jadon to fill. Dortmund had so much confidence in Jadon that they gave him Dembélé's squad number: 7.

A number any young trickster would love to possess.

Jadon leant back in his reclining airplane seat and removed his headphones. He looked out of the window in wonder. Below, he saw a city at night twinkling like a starry sky with all of its lights and life.

The city of Dortmund is one that lives and breathes football. Jadon was no longer just another young academy prospect. He would be playing in front of 80,000+ fans at the (Westfalenstadion) Signal Iduna Park. This is the largest football stadium in Germany, with its intimidating yellow spires and famous 'yellow wall': a well-known name for one of the most incredible sights in world football. 25,000 fans stand behind one of the goals, and with their yellow-and-black banners they create a stunning but terrifying sight for opposition teams to behold.

The time for quiet celebrations was over. It was time for the sound of thousands cheering his name. Time for the city of Dortmund to meet Jadon Sancho.

★ FOOTBALL RISING STARS ★

It would not take too long for the Dortmund fans to see their new player. The moment came in the 83rd minute of a tie between Borussia Dortmund and Eintracht Frankfurt. The score was 2-2. Maximilian Philip had suffered an injury and needed to come off the pitch. Jadon was warming up on the touchline. He pulled his foot behind him and stretched. As he stood on one foot, he looked around the stadium and saw over 80,000 fans cheering on his new team. The Dortmund manager at the time, Peter Bosz, managed to catch

★ JADON SANCHO ★

Jadon's attention with a flailing hand. It was not easy to make himself heard over 80,000 fans who were singing and shouting.

He beckoned Jadon over.

'It's your time,' he said. 'You can do this.'

The ball ran out of play and Jadon was standing by the touchline. The assistant held up the number board and it flashed '7'. Philip came off the pitch and patted Jadon on the shoulder. Not once had an English player graced the Borussia Dortmund pitch. This was an incredible moment for both Jadon and the history books. Jadon looked up to the sky as if thanking the heavens for the opportunity to play. Then he sprinted onto the pitch. The announcer shouted his name and the fans roared, adding extra life into an already fierce game.

In his first ten minutes of professional football, Jadon could not win the game for the team. He had a half-chance that was brilliantly saved by the imposing Finnish goalkeeper Lukáš Hrádecký. But in the coming weeks, during his first full team debut, Jadon would start to fulfil his potential.

Wolfsburg were the opponents, and although the game ended as a scoreless draw, there was no denying that Jadon was a talented player. He shone throughout the game against an experienced and talented side.

In the 53rd minute, he struck a fearsome shot that rattled the post of the opposition's goal. The fans were excited following the media hype and stories about this young English starlet. Now they had proof on the pitch. It was clear that this teenager, from a country hundreds of miles away, was going to be a fan favourite at Borussia Dortmund.

In his first season at the club, Jadon did not get as much game time as first promised. With tough competition, from experienced professionals, he made only fourteen appearances. It was an incredible achievement for a 17-year-old. But of course, for a player with desire and ambition, this needed to improve.

★ JADON SANCHO ★

Halfway through the season, after a string of poor performances, Peter Bosz was replaced by Peter Stöger as the manager. However, Stöger only lasted six months in the job. It was towards the latter part of the season, during Stöger's short reign, when it was clear that things were starting to click. In a 4-0 victory over Bayer 04 Leverkusen, Jadon was nothing short of unstoppable. Not only did he grab his first professional goal for the team, but he also assisted a further two of the goals scored in the match.

After scoring his goal in front of the thousands of screaming fans, Jadon ran to the corner, kissed his badge and leapt into the air in celebration. This amazing performance was a marker and a warning to their rivals.

In the summer, a former Swiss international player and clever tactician, Lucien Favre, started to bring the best out of Jadon. Under a new manager who trusted him, and with the confidence of the team, he had everything he needed to take the league by storm the following season ...

7
THE ASSIST KING

Bayern Munich, one of Borussia Dortmund's rivals, are the most successful team in the history of the Bundesliga. Since the league's creation, Bayern have won thirty Bundesliga titles, while Borussia Dortmund have five. This is the joint-second highest total with Borussia Mönchengladbach.

During Jadon's first year, this trend of domination continued. Bayern picked up their fifth Bundesliga title in a row and were looking unstoppable. In a league so greatly dominated by one team, it would take a lot to upset the balance.

However, the Bundesliga had not yet met the 2018/2019 edition of Jadon Sancho. Here was a young player from a faraway land, keen to steal Bayern's crown.

One of Dortmund's most famous campaigns in recent history started

★ JADON SANCHO ★

at Signal Iduna Park on the 26th of August 2018. Following a poor season in which they finished fourth, twenty-nine points behind the champions, Bayern, Dortmund were ready to put the past behind them and focus on the present.

The season kicked-off in a stadium packed with fans roaring, singing and chanting to push their team to the next level. Large black-and-yellow flags with the club's badge waved in the summer breeze around the stadium.

The referee blew his whistle and the dream season for Dortmund got off to the worst possible start. A mere thirty-one seconds into the match, RB Leipzig scored the opening goal. Jean-Kévin Augustin slotted the ball into the Dortmund net, and the excitement, noise and optimism of the Dortmund fans was momentarily silenced.

But Dortmund did not let this early setback define them. Thanks to goals from Mahmoud Dahoud, a Marcel Sabitzer own goal and an acrobatic Axel Witsel overhead kick, they found themselves 3-1 up at half-time.

In the second half, Jadon ran down the left wing. He humbled the Leipzig defence and sent a careful pass into the path of club captain Marco Reus. *Goal!* He smashed the ball into the net, setting Dortmund and Jadon off to the perfect start.

Dortmund went unbeaten for fifteen games in the Bundesliga. But a famous match against the reigning champions Bayern was a clear sign that this year wouldn't be an easy stroll to the title.

Bayern grabbed the first goal of the game via a Robert Lewandowski header and made their way into half-time with the lead. Buoyed by the booming Dortmund crowd, Jadon left the defenders behind with his blistering pace and sent a through ball to Reus, who was brought down by Manuel Neuer.

He'd won a penalty.

Reus calmly ran up to the ball and smashed it into the right of the goal.

Later, Bayern reclaimed the lead with another Lewandowski header. But a stunning volley from Reus levelled the game with hardly any time to spare.

Battling as hard as he could, and running with every ounce of energy

★ JADON SANCHO ★

he had left, Jadon made a tackle in his own half. He fed the ball to Reus who backheeled the ball to Witsel. Witsel ran into Bayern's half and played a through ball to Paco Alcácer. He charged through on goal. Neuer rushed towards him, and he was going to close down the space. Was the chance over?

Alcácer dinked the ball over him.

He'd done it!

The crowd erupted and drinks were launched into the air, spraying everyone in the stadium.

★ **FOOTBALL RISING STARS** ★

But no one cared. They were about to win *Der Klassiker* – the name given to the fierce matches between these two teams. The Dortmund fans couldn't have been happier.

Despite this incredible victory, it would not be the year for Dortmund to steal the title. Bayern had not been far away all season. They would end up winning the league on the final day with a two-point cushion. No club had run Bayern this close for the title in years, and it was down in part to Jadon's brilliance. It was in this season that he became known as one

of the best assisters in world football. He made thirty-four appearances in the league, assisted seventeen goals and scored twelve. It was a tally that would delight even experienced player, let alone an 18-year-old still in development.

The 2019/2020 season followed a similar course. Bayern Munich once again won the division, and Borussia Dortmund took second place. Jadon continued his hot streak of form and got himself both seventeen goals and seventeen assists. Compared to his starting season, it was now never in doubt: if Borussia Dortmund were playing, Jadon's name would be one of the first on the team sheet.

Dortmund was no longer a scary city in the faraway reaches of a foreign country. With an incredible team bond, and a guiding hand from Lucien Favre, it was starting to look like Jadon's new home.

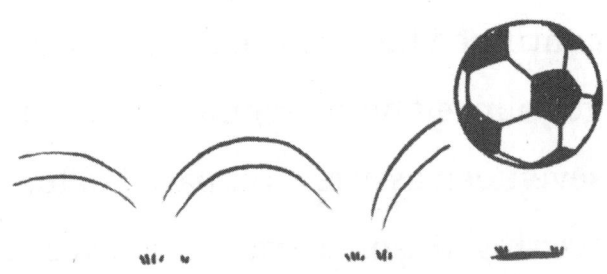

8
THE THREE LIONS

As a child, Jadon would sit with friends watching England play. On one occasion, the national team were playing in a World Cup. There were stars like Wayne Rooney, Steven Gerrard and Frank Lampard. They were all lined up and singing the national anthem. They had their hands on their chests and their heads held high as they belted out the words. Jadon watched as the camera panned across them, and he wondered what it would be like to be there. To play for England and represent his country. He daydreamed about being the next player on screen. About looking across the stadium filled with thousands upon thousands of fans with hopes and dreams of victory.

'That's going to be me one day,' said Jadon, under his breath.

★ JADON SANCHO ★

To play professional football is incredible. To be called up to play on the national development team is an honour. But to be selected for the senior national team is nothing short of a lifetime achievement. It's a phone call that any player will dream about. It's a phone call that can bring grown men to tears.

During Jadon's brilliant campaign with Dortmund, he captured not only the imagination of the German  leagues but of the entire world. With his pace, drive and talent, it was time for him to be tested on the international stage.

Jadon had just finished training and was in the locker room. After changing and getting ready to go home, he checked his phone. There was a message from an unknown number. He opened it and had to rub his eyes in disbelief as he read it. It was a message inviting him to join the squad for the upcoming England matches.

He would be joining the twenty-five-man squad to face Croatia and Spain in the first season of the Nations League. He wouldn't be making his

★ JADON SANCHO ★

debut in dead-rubber friendlies, but in an intense new tournament where every point mattered.

Jadon arrived at St George's Park in a taxi with his close friend Reiss Nelson. Reiss hadn't been called up for the seniors, but had instead been called up to play for the England U21 side. Jadon was kitted out in the new England tracksuit and was carrying his boots and clothes in a black and yellow Dortmund suitcase. He was met by a greeting team who directed him to where he'd be staying before they flew out to Croatia.

Jadon wasn't the only new starter. This was also the first international call-up for James Maddison and Mason Mount. He would be getting used to playing against stars week in and week out, training with England regulars such as Harry Kane, Jordan Henderson and Sterling. Only a few years ago he was watching such players on TV!

Like in his standout performances in the U17 European Championships, it was against Croatia that Jadon earned his first ever international cap.

★ JADON SANCHO ★

However, the game happened in an unusual way. The match was played without a crowd, as Croatia were being punished following anti-Semitic actions by a small group of fans. Despite the stadium being empty, millions tuned in to watch on TV. Jadon became the first player born in this millennium to represent England.

In the 77th minute, the game was level at 0-0. Without fans, every kick, shout and thump of the ball could be heard. Gareth Southgate asked Jadon to warm up, and he came on for a tiring Sterling.

Jadon had always admired Sterling, and now he was going to be the one replacing him on the pitch. His first appearance went by in a flash. He impressed with his darting runs, but in such a short space of time was unable to make a big difference. The game ended at 0-0, and England took a point from the game.

It was in his eighth appearance for The Three Lions that Jadon got his first goal. England were playing Kosovo in a qualifying match for the European Championships in 2021. Jadon's first important contribution

JADON SANCHO

was sprinting down the side of the opposition's box and drilling the ball across the six-yard line. The ball cannoned into the goal, off an unfortunate defender. Although it was classed as an own goal, Jadon was still credited with an assist.

Jadon's first goal was a gift from Sterling. The tricky winger sprinted across the pitch and passed the ball to Jadon inside the box. He pulled away to the right before slotting the ball into the back of the net. Jadon jogged towards the fans and the corner of the pitch with an enormous smile on his face, and his eyes almost closed. He was taking in the fact that he'd just scored his first ever goal for England. The Wembley crowd roared as he kissed the badge and celebrated with them.

It wasn't just the one goal that Jadon got in this game. Once again, Sterling provided the assist with a dazzling run down the left wing. He guided the ball into Jadon's path for an easy tap in. It was Jadon's second goal for England. The team won the qualifier 5-3 and went on to qualify for the European Championships.

★ **JADON SANCHO** ★

The question now was, would Jadon Sancho be in Gareth Southgate's squad by the time the major competition arrived? Would he not only represent England in a qualifier, but get the chance to represent his country in a major international tournament?

9
THE CHAMPIONS LEAGUE

Imagine challenging for a league title, playing for an international team and walking out to the sound of the Champions League anthem. Before Jadon had even turned 20, he'd accomplished all three. These were three objectives any seasoned professional would dream of achieving.

It was during Jadon's breakthrough season in 2018/2019 that he first graced the Champions League pitch. He earned his debut away to Club Brugge in Belgium. There, the team started the group stages off with a 0-1 away win. He went on to grab his first assist away at AS Monaco and his first goal in a 4-0 thrashing of Atlético Madrid. However, his most anticipated game of the season was the round of

16 tie against Tottenham Hotspur. For the first time in his club career, Jadon was getting the chance to play where it all started. He would get to play in front of his friends and family in London.

Jadon was standing in the Wembley tunnel and the atmosphere was charged. This was an important Champions League knock-out match. It was the first of two match legs, and a night that football fans craved. Studs scratched against the tunnel floor and players clapped and called their teammates to action.

★ JADON SANCHO ★

The opponents' captain, Harry Kane, tried to motivate his team.

'Let's go, lads!' he shouted.

Jadon's captain, Reus, did the same, before they followed the referees into an atmospheric Wembley stadium. The Champions League anthem boomed across the ground as the players made their way onto the grass. Scattered across the stadium, Jadon's family and friends were watching on proudly. He would be playing an important match less than fifteen miles away from where he grew up.

Only a short distance from the cages, streets and parks where he had first kicked a football.

Jadon's homecoming did not turn out the way he wanted. Dortmund lost 3-0 to an inspired Tottenham side that would in fact make it all the way to the final. In the following season, it was a familiar story. Despite the exceptional addition of the Norwegian superstar Erling Braut Haaland, Dortmund were knocked out at the round of 16 again. This time it was a much closer game after defeating PSG at home 2-1. They then

★ JADON SANCHO ★

lost the second tie in Paris 2-0 and were knocked out of the competition.

Despite these setbacks, it was still an achievement to make it that far into the competition. And it was an incredible feat to be competing, and not looking out of place, against the world's best football players.

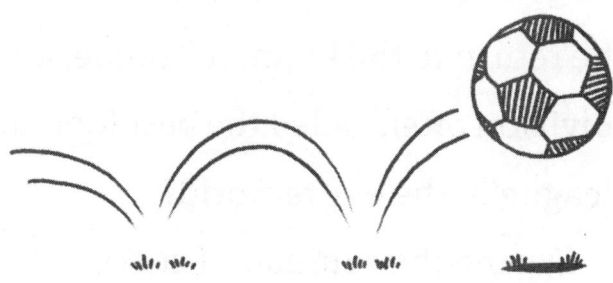

RETURN TO MANCHESTER?

As soon as Jadon left England, there was always going to be a question lingering over his head. When would he return to the Premier League, a division often called the best football league in the entire world?

During the summer of 2020,

★ JADON SANCHO ★

the biggest story of the transfer market was the Jadon Sancho saga. Following his unusual move to Dortmund as a teenager, and now after three seasons with the German side, his profile had gone from strength to strength. Now, as an England regular, Jadon frequently drew attention from the press and media in his home country.

Rumours started to swirl that a certain club in Manchester was after his signature. It wouldn't be a reunion with the sky blue of Manchester City, but instead a potential move to their great rivals: Manchester United.

In recent history it was clear to see that Manchester City were now the leading team in Manchester. Manchester United had enjoyed decades of dominance as the most decorated club in English football. Yet after their celebrated manager Sir Alex Ferguson retired in 2013, the club had started to slowly decline. Manchester City, a club with a much less decorated past, took this as their opportunity to step out of their rival's shadow. Disgusted with City's

★ JADON SANCHO ★

successes, Manchester United needed to change. They brought in a former player, Ole Gunnar Solskjær, as the manager of the side in an attempt to take back their crown as the best team in Manchester.

Despite the inspired signing of Portuguese attacking midfielder Bruno Fernandes, United were still behind their rivals. What they needed was a star. And from this want and desire came a transfer saga that would last until the final day of the transfer window on October 5th, 2020.

Borussia Dortmund were not very willing to lose one of their best players. But in modern football it's not always about what the club wants. It's also about the desires and motivations of the player. Also, following the extraordinary year that saw the spread of the COVID-19 pandemic, the financial strength of every club in the world was lessened. Jadon had enjoyed an incredible career so far in Dortmund. As far as the hopes of the team went, there were still milestones to achieve. He had not yet won a trophy with

★ JADON SANCHO ★

Borussia Dortmund, and a player's career can often be judged by the amount of medals and awards in their cabinet. If Jadon decided to leave now, would he have regrets about not winning anything with Dortmund?

Yet the pull to Manchester was a strong one. There he would be the poster boy for one of the most famous clubs in the world, and he would be returning to his home country. He'd be closer to friends and family, in a country where he could speak the language fluently, and have a chance to play in the Premier League.

★ FOOTBALL RISING STARS ★

No matter what the outcome, Jadon Sancho was going to be a leading football player in the 2020/2021 season. It just wasn't decided yet in what colour kit and in what country he would be playing.

During the summer, Jadon flew out to Ibiza for a holiday so he could flick the football switch off in his brain and take a well-deserved break. He stood on the back of a yacht in the glaring sun. Music blasted from speakers as his close friends enjoyed a day to remember. Jadon dipped his feet in the cool sea while sitting on the yacht's steps. He strapped a pair of goggles and a snorkel to his face and plunged into the water. He floated and peered down at the sea floor beneath him. He saw rocks, sand and the occasional fish swimming by. The loud noise of the music and chatter was gone. All he could hear was the soothing sound of the sea around him.

While Jadon was enjoying life in Ibiza, negotiations between Dortmund and United continued. Dortmund were clear that they

★ FOOTBALL RISING STARS ★

wanted to receive a fee in excess of €120 million for their star player. But Manchester United did not want to pay that much and tried to negotiate a cheaper deal. This transfer talk continued well into the start of the new season. It lasted until the final day of the transfer window. As the weeks, days and hours passed, the question on every football fan's mind was whether Jadon Sancho would be making the big money move to Manchester United.

On October 5th, 2020, millions of football fans checked their phones and

★ JADON SANCHO ★

tuned in to news channels to see who their club would be signing this year.

The clock struck 11PM and the transfer window closed.

Jadon Sancho's incredible Bundesliga journey was far from finished.

A ROLE MODEL AT DORTMUND

After a summer filled with speculation and rumours, Jadon tried to clear his mind for the 2020/2021 season. He was not involved in a big money transfer, but he was going to be needed to support an incoming transfer. Borussia Dortmund had picked up another promising English starlet: Jude Bellingham. Bellingham was only 17 years old and had previously played in the English second tier. Now he was a first team player for Borussia Dortmund. At the young age of 17, the midfielder's fee set a world record as he was purchased for just under £21 million. There was no one better placed than Jadon Sancho to understand and relate to the teenager.

On the first day back for pre-season, Jadon was excited for Jude to join training. He sat in the driver's seat of his car and eagerly watched the players arrive. He didn't have to wait too long before he saw Jude enter the car park. As he spotted him, Jadon opened his car door.

'My guy!' called Jadon.

'Hey, Jadon!' said Jude.

The two of them hugged.

'I'm so glad to finally be here,' said Jude. 'This summer has been dragging on!'

'It's been a mad one,' said Jadon.

★ JADON SANCHO ★

'How about I give you a tour?'

Jadon took Jude under his wing and helped him get used to life in a new country at such a young age. But equally, having Jude around was important for Jadon too. Having another native English speaker, who had experienced many of the same things that he had, was comforting.

As much as Jadon helped Jude to settle, Jude's presence helped Jadon to clear his mind following a wild summer of ups and downs.

But despite his best efforts, Jadon was unable to fully shake off the stress of his summer. He struggled as the season kicked off. Borussia Dortmund started the season slowly, well below the high expectations that were now put on the team. It didn't help matters when Jadon picked up a thigh injury during the season. It caused him to miss six matches in a row. However, with all the efforts of the team, Dortmund started to improve, winning seven

★ JADON SANCHO ★

matches in a row at the end of the season to finish a respectable third place. Dortmund earned Champions League qualification when, at times, it seemed that they were going to miss out. Despite falling below his exceedingly high expectations, Jadon still scored eight goals and provided thirteen assists.

While their Bundesliga campaign hadn't gone to plan, Jadon and Dortmund had found hope in the DFB-Pokal: Germany's knock-out cup competition. Dortmund made it all the way to the final, with only

RB Leipzig standing in the way of a cup triumph. The heavyweight clash, between two top sides, kicked off in the Olympiastadion in Berlin.

It didn't take Jadon long to make his mark in this important fixture. In the 5th minute of the match, he received the ball from Dahoud. Jadon, with a wall of defenders in front of him, snuck into the box. The defenders could only watch as Jadon released an unstoppable strike. The ball curled towards the right of the goal and left the goalkeeper with nothing to do but stretch his arms out as far as he could. But the strike was too powerful. *Goal!* Jadon Sancho had put Borussia Dortmund into the lead.

This early goal set a blistering pace for the match, and in the 28th minute Haaland put Dortmund 2-0 up. Just before half-time, Jadon had another chance. Reus had made a run beyond the defence and was clear. As he reached the box, the opposition goalkeeper narrowed the target, but Jadon sprinted to catch up with his captain. Reus fed the ball to Jadon, who pretended to shoot with his right. This confused a defender and caused him to slip. Jadon then calmly passed the ball into an open net with his left to make it 3-0 heading into half-time.

RB Leipzig were able to grab a goal back in the second half, with an impressive long-distance strike from Dani Olmo. However, Haaland put the cherry on top of the sweetest scoreline, and put Dortmund 4-1 up in the 87th minute. Despite what had appeared to be a Bundesliga season to forget, Borussia Dortmund had claimed their first piece of silverware in four years. And after four years with Dortmund, Jadon had earned his first ever professional trophy.

As the season came to a close and summer began, the transfer rumour mill started once again. Many experts and fans wondered whether this had been Jadon's last year as a Dortmund player, and would be the summer that he took the next step in his career.

But before any of these rumours could be addressed, there was a small matter that needed to be dealt with.

The delayed Euro 2020 tournament was taking place during the summer of 2021. Was Jadon going to be one of the names included in the squad? Was he about to head to his first ever major international tournament?

12
THE RED DEVILS

The 2020/2021 season was over, but Jadon's summer holiday had to wait. With his impressive return to form, Jadon was included in Gareth Southgate's final England squad for Euro 2020. He was joining up with the national team in the hope of leading England to a trophy for the first time since 1966.

England progressed from Group D with two victories and a draw. They beat Croatia and Czech Republic, but drew with a fellow British side Scotland. England won their group, which meant a round of 16 tie against Germany. The young German team had survived Group F, the so-called 'Group of Death', finishing in second place. But thanks to the England team's incredible sense of unity,

★ JADON SANCHO ★

they were able to triumph against Germany at Wembley. This set up a quarter final against Ukraine.

While away with England, Jadon focussed on his international duties. For the summer, his priority was winning a trophy with England, and nothing else. However, the same could not be said for Borussia Dortmund and Manchester United. Once more, the Red Devils wanted to bring Jadon to their club. Although a deal had failed in 2020, this time an agreement was edging closer than it had ever been before. Was this the summer when Jadon would return to England?

The answer came as Jadon was pedalling away on an exercise bike surrounded by his teammates. Luke Shaw was to his left and Marcus Rashford was to his right. In front of them, Sterling and Henderson were firing basketballs at a hoop. As Jadon watched them play, he felt his phone vibrating in his shorts pocket. It was his agent. He jumped off the bike and headed outside.

'Jadon, are you sitting comfortably? I've got some pretty exciting news!'

★ JADON SANCHO ★

said his agent. 'A fee's been agreed – an offer of £73 million. Of course, you'll need to pass a medical after the tournament, and we'll need to finalise your contract. But other than that, you're swapping Dortmund for Manchester.'

Jadon leant against the wall and took in the news. Although he was happy to have a new opportunity with a team as historic as Manchester United, it was mixed with a pang of sadness.

He'd loved his time at Dortmund. He was sorry

to be leaving a team that had done so much for him. But above all, he was glad to be heading home.

'That's amazing,' said Jadon. 'Thank you. We did it this time! I'd best get back to training.'

'No worries,' said his agent. '"And Sancho scores for Manchester United!" Sounds good, doesn't it?'

'It certainly does,' laughed Jadon.

Jadon burst back into the gym and rushed over to Shaw and Rashford.

'Why are you grinning like the cat who got the cream?' asked Rashford.

Jadon hopped back on his bike

with a laugh. 'Because we're teammates at club level now too. I'm signing for United!'

13
ROAD TO QATAR 2022

Jadon's positive attitude and hard work led to him being named in the starting lineup for the quarter-final against Ukraine. The decision to include Sancho was met with excitement from the nation's fans, as they'd wanted to see more of their

★ JADON SANCHO ★

talented attacker. They were not left disappointed when Jadon played his part in a 0-4 victory against Ukraine. It was the team's largest win of the tournament and by far the most dominant. Goals from Kane, Henderson and Harry Maguire sent England through to the semi-final to play Denmark.

Jadon was not selected to play against the Danes, but England still progressed against a determined side.

The opposition took the lead in the 30th minute thanks to an unstoppable free kick by Mikkel Damsgaard. England soon replied with a goal of their own. Fellow rising star Bukayo Saka made a darting run into the penalty box and fired the ball across goal. In an attempt to clear it, Denmark's captain, Simon Kjær, stuck out a leg, but could only divert it into the back of his net. It was an own goal! The score was 1-1.

Neither side could find a winner within ninety minutes, and so extra time was needed. Jadon watched on from the bench nervously as the minutes swiftly passed him by.

★ JADON SANCHO ★

He moved to the edge of his seat as Sterling zipped into Denmark's penalty area. He was clipped by not just one defender but two. Jadon leapt from his seat.

'It's a penalty!' he shouted. 'He tripped him!'

The referee brought his whistle to his mouth and pointed to the spot. The fans in the Wembley stadium went wild, knowing that this was their chance to win the game.

Kane, England's much-loved captain, took the ball and prepared to take the spot kick. This could be the goal to send England to their first final in fifty-five years. Kane ran up to the ball and struck it to the right. Denmark's goalkeeper, Kasper Schmeichel, reached out his gloves and saved it. But it rebounded into the penalty area, and Kane knew exactly what to do. The striker swept the ball into the net. *Goal!* Wembley erupted, and Jadon celebrated with the other substitutes as if he'd scored himself.

England held on, and the team progressed past an exhausted but brave Denmark side. It was official,

★ JADON SANCHO ★

England were one of the teams in the final. But to lift the trophy, they needed to defeat Italy.

England's final got off to the perfect start when Shaw scored early in the game. Italy equalised in the second half thanks to their centre back Leonardo Bonucci. The Italian defender prodded the ball into the net following a goalmouth scramble, after a corner. Neither team managed to score in ninety minutes, or even in extra time.

As with so many of England's past knock-out matches, this final was to be settled by penalties. As one of the best technical players in the team, Jadon was brought onto the pitch as a substitute in the final minutes of the match. He came on alongside Rashford as one of the five nominated penalty-takers. However, a night of such promise soon turned into one of heartbreak. Jadon's penalty was saved, as were those of his teammates Rashford and Saka.

England were defeated.

The team were devastated that they'd come so close to winning the trophy, only to be returning home with runners up medals instead. But this tournament wasn't all about winning. Jadon had played his part in a team that had fed the hopes and dreams of football fans across the country. He had been in the most successful England team since 1966 – a team that had reached the final of a major international competition. This was an incredible achievement for any footballer, let alone one only at the start of his career.

At only 21 years old, Jadon had already experienced a lot for a young footballer. He'd traded Kennington streets for professional pitches and football cages for Wembley stadium. He'd turned scoring goals in empty parking lots into scoring winners in front of tens of thousands of adoring fans. He never once forgot his roots and the people who'd helped him when he needed them the most. He'd changed greatly from the young boy who arrived at Watford, to the academy prospect at Manchester City, to the star struck teenager who'd traded England for Germany. But despite all of these changes, one thing

JADON SANCHO

had always remained the same: his passion for football.

Jadon may not have been able to bring the trophy home from the European Championships, but during his career he had broken records and scored goals galore. With his undeniable talent, there were going to be many chances for silverware in the future. Perhaps Jadon Sancho would be part of a World Cup winning team at Qatar 2022.

But first Jadon had something else to look forward to. He was coming home. He was returning to

Manchester and, better yet, to a club in need of a hero. With Jadon's help, could Manchester United finally awaken from their slumber and battle their way to the throne of English football once again?